24 LESSONS ON ENTREPRENEURSH IP

BY:

MANSA MUHAMMAD

©2014 Timbuctoo Publishing

TABLE OF CONTENTS

INTRODUCTION

Today, we exist within a global economy. The global economy is interconnected and interdependent. Many people believe that a globally interconnected and inter-dependent economy is unsustainable. However, this is the world we've created through technology and necessity. We are far from living in the Stone Age, yet we could thrust ourselves back into that era if we lose these techniques. Technology has brought humanity closer together despite being separated by several thousand miles. We are just one click away from each other through the power of the Internet and other innovative technologies. As an American, our economy is apparently suffering from staggering amounts of debt. It is a reality that job security will never be as it used to be. The destruction of pension plans and retirement programs occurred because of the housing bubble bursting in 2008. Job security will never return to its former glory. At least not in the form we once knew it to be. Major U.S. Companies have already exported many of their available jobs to foreign countries. The remaining positions pay wages that are below the standard of living.

The Young Generation of America cannot look towards social security as a retirement plan as it will have no more funds available by the time, they reach their senior years. The college market holds very little promise as well. Many college graduates are finding it more and more difficult to find decent-paying jobs to sufficiently make a living. College tuition is already costly, and now it's becoming extremely unaffordable. Graduates are swamped with student loan debts and often fall into default, making life more difficult to cope with. There is no longer a middle class or working class in America; instead, there is the working poor. The term working poor describes most American lives today. Many people are barely getting by.

Even two-person households feel the strain of making ends meet. Young people in America, in large numbers, are moving back home with their parents. The Home foreclosures crisis has created a class of Americans who strictly rent. Being a homeowner is no longer the goal for many Americans, and the situation doesn't seem to be getting better anytime soon, especially for those at the lower rungs of society. The gap between rich and poor has soared through the roof, and the trend will not slow down anytime soon. Where has all the wealth gone? Well, wealth is never destroyed but merely transferred from one to the other or from here to there.

The wealth of this world developed during the formation of the Earth. Therefore, it is impossible to create more wealth; in the sense that it comes from nothing. The wealth of this Earth has been extracted and transferred from one group to the next throughout the history of our existence.

Most people do not know how to create value so that they can obtain wealth from the very fabric of society. I will go deeper into many of these concepts in later degrees. For now, make a note that what is lacking in this country is the spirit and drive of entrepreneurship. Other factors are stifling the growth of prosperity, but most of it has to do with personal responsibility and the inability to be self-motivated, especially for those living in America. There is always an opportunity to come from nothing to something in America. That is the premise of the American Dream. It is time for those who are either suffering from poverty, the possibility of becoming impoverished, or those who are trying to escape mediocrity to suck it up and begin to diligently create a plan that can lead them to the life they want.

America has been teaching its youth how to become worker drones instead of masters of their fate. So many young people are suffering from debt from student loans and have no hopes for a future worth anything beyond being a slave to their nine to five jobs if they are lucky to find or get one. While it is true that we all cannot be bosses, the reality is that there is an imbalance between people looking for jobs and those who are creating them. You must realize that it is entrepreneurs who create jobs for those who have decided that their fate is to be a worker. There is most certainly a correlation between capital being accessible to entrepreneurs and the lack of new job creation. However, as the old saying goes, "where there is a will, there is a way." In this globalized economy, there is always an opportunity to extract capital from the most unlikely places to finance and fund new ventures. The truth of the matter is that there has been a lack of education about how the entrepreneurial world works.

Knowledge is indeed power, and the more you know, the more you can do.

It is time for the American people to become entrepreneurs. The masses that took the advice of their elders are finding out that this path does not lead to success and security as it did many years ago. Going to college or seeking higher education should never be shunned by anyone, especially the youth of America. However, viewing it as the only route to success isn't wise. Education without a purpose isn't beneficial when one cannot put that training to use practically.

Education etymologically means to train. So apparently, when you are getting an education, you are getting prepared for a specific task, duty, or purpose. This is why by the time you get to college; you must choose a subject you will major or minor. Perhaps this isn't a bad thing, nor is it a good thing, but it should be understood precisely for what it is, which is training for a specific task, or duty, nothing more and nothing less. Knowledge is different from education. Many people believe that getting an education is about learning and gaining experience. While it contains those two elements, its primary purpose is training people. Mostly training that teaches people how to become a worker drone for someone else. There isn't anything wrong with the average working person who earns an honest wage. However, one should take note that being such a person directly puts someone else in control of your financial and economic well-being. Education alone doesn't teach a person how to become an entrepreneur. How to create jobs? Or how to be their boss?

Although we need society to provide adequate training so that we can all function at a fundamental level, problems develop when everyone gets shuffled into this system with the intent of being a worker drone; it has caused a severe imbalance in the general marketplace. Simply put, everyone has been taught to get a job, but no one has the education on how to create jobs. Even though Ivy League Universities provide the most proficient education, it still does not teach their student body to become job creators. Many Ivy League graduates cannot find jobs themselves. Most are finding jobs through referrals from family and friends It is merely pure insanity for such a significant portion of the American youth to continue to hold on to the idea that their primary focus should be graduating from college and getting a job. Albert Einstein once said, "insanity doing the same thing repeatedly and expecting different results."

There are some things politically that must happen to increase job creation, but politicians are not being pressured to do such things because most people are concerned with finding a job in the existing job market instead of urging their politicians to create and implement policies that are conducive to entrepreneurs and small businesses. The reality facing the American Youth today is that they must turn away and shun the old ideas of becoming a worker drone while toiling and laboring to make someone else rich. They must instead turn inwards and mine their inner being for the wealth within themselves and share it with the world. There are too many opportunities that many young Americans have missed because of the lack of knowledge and proper perspective on life.

The lack of view can keep a person in total blindness about what exists and what doesn't. We stand at the precipice of enormous change in our world; this will be negative for some and positive for others, but it will all depend on your perspective. It all depends on whether you are an optimist, pessimist, idealist, realist, or opportunist. The best one to me is a little of all. Being able to have the perspective of these entire mentalities can and will prepare you to make the best decisions possible regarding the financial future of your life. Without proper perspective, a person is lost to the ideologies of others, lacking their thoughts on the subject or issues. Losing individual perspectives creates a dependent mentality, which perpetuates the habit of blaming others for one's failures or shortcomings. Had one had their unique view and original thoughts on a matter, they would be anxious to live and die by their ideologies and realities, not to the point of delusions, but to the limit of trusting in one's own ability to make the proper decisions for themselves.

The real problems that plague young Americans are their lack of ambition and reliance on the government to solve their problems because they're used to being coddled. The truth of the matter is that Young Americans must become familiar with entrepreneurship. Entrepreneurship is the craft of pushing your way forward to success. Young Americans must learn to apply the solutions to an entrepreneur's mentality, so they may move forward toward the success they seek and desire. I establish some preliminary lessons in this book, which will show you how to do just that. Positive thinking is necessary and should be a standard application in the thought processes of anyone striving for success. However, this book will not focus on positive thinking and get-rich-quick schemes. There aren't any shortcuts to success, and it is up to you to design your roadmap to achieve the kind of success you want. I wish there were a way to get rich quickly that someone packaged into a step-by-step process, but the truth tells us that the road to success has many pitfalls, setbacks, and detours. The key lies in determination, dedication, and discipline. Without those three attributes, a person can never attain the level of success one is striving to reach. I will provide you with a quick plan of action and a way to comprehensively employ sound reasoning to achieve the desired results and outcomes. This book will show you how to apply the intangibles to your thought process and business acumen to get ahead on your road to success. Many people are unaware of what a person must do to achieve success, but it is all the little things that make the most significant difference in whether you succeed or fail.

The nuances are crucial when trying to achieve the goals you set for yourself. Without doing the little things, you can best believe you will almost always fail or be hindered in your progress. This book will also show you how to use business entities to maneuver through this global economy on a broad and fundamental level. The key to understanding what entrepreneurship is and how to activate its knowledge, a person must understand the essential nature of what business entities are and how they operate within the legal system and context of the global economy. A significant yet subtle mental adjustment must be made on your part when seeking to apply this information. Aspiring entrepreneurs must be more interested in learning about systems and processes, as well as attaining vital knowledge that would be instrumental in achieving their goals. You must be ready and willing to get knowledge at all costs.

You must be willing to put an end to your days of being a worker drone and building someone else's commercial empire. You must be prepared to invest lots of time and energy into bettering yourself so that you make better decisions and choices in your business affairs. A simple principle to live by is the more you know, the more you can do, and while living in this age of information, where information is the most asset in today's world.

Knowing and understanding that knowledge reigns supreme over nearly everyone is vital. General information must be thoroughly processed and examined before it is determined to be accurate information. Therefore, you should use your brain more than you ever have before because exact details coupled with correct action will make the difference between success and failure. This book will touch on some very technical aspects of entrepreneurship as it relates to the global economy and emerging industries and markets. Many times when people decide to start businesses. They will make the decision using their emotions to determine what will sell or what would be a good business to start; based on their habits as a consumer. Never taking into consideration the nature of the market they are entering; they lunge themselves into that market and become quickly discouraged because they never considered the variables and difficulties that existed within that market.

They could have easily avoided many of the mistakes that led to their discouragement; had they thoroughly researched the market they were entering. Many businesses fail because they lack patience, and many companies fail before they get started. A lot of people are anxious to make money fast, and it is possible to do so in today's global economy. Achieve success with careful planning based on correct information. This process of planning and market research can take up to months and maybe even years (depending on what you are trying to achieve) to beautifully execute a plan that can make you fast and easy money.

The key is that you will have to work hard mentally. In most cases, the old way of doing things requires you to work hard physically. With the power of the internet, it is much easier to bring your product or service to market to consumers, especially with the advent of social media.

People mostly set themselves up for failure if they seek to make money quickly, without maximum planning, application, and effort. You must meet the proper requirements and prerequisites to achieve success. Success has a mathematical trajectory, which is guaranteed to reach its mark. Use that precise formula for success, for it will be the only way you can solidify the victory in your own life.

1st LESSON: WHAT IS AN ENTREPRENEUR?

An entrepreneur prides himself or herself on being able to create commercial entities whenever they see an opportunity to make money. Creating business entities is a very ancient tradition, which until 100 or so years ago was only available to Sovereigns, Nobles, and high-status Merchants, and not to the Common Folk and Peasant class of people. Usually, Kings or Queens, i.e., Sovereigns, are chartered entities. They did this so that the interested parties could do business on behalf of one or more people and represent them in business decisions where they weren't available. A Corporation is a specific type of entity; its main feature is surviving its physical members' death and existence in perpetuity. Corporations are like mini governments. In fact, Corporations operate in the same manner as governments do, with the exception that Corporations usually don't create laws for the public; instead, they develop by-laws for the internal governing of their employees and executives.

There are various types of legal entities, and Corporations are just one of them. Partnerships, Limited Liability Companies, and unincorporated companies. Out of these different kinds of businesses, the Corporation (of which there are two, the "C" & "S" corporation) is the more widely used form of entity; when it comes to fortune 500 companies because of the nature of its set up is in alignment with publicly traded companies. The Limited Liability Company is undoubtedly a prevalent form of entity that a lot of entrepreneurs utilize. LLCs are a hybrid type of entity, consisting of elements relative to a C Corporation and a Partnership.

LLCs have a lighter paperwork load than that of a corporation but also allow you to maneuver the seas of commerce as if you are a partnership with the benefits of a corporation. You should consult with a specialized attorney for more information. However, independent research and studies go a very long way in helping you build a working knowledge base about entities in their various forms and usage.

It is a foundational principle that all entrepreneurs and those aspiring to be so familiarized themselves at best, with the nature and application of commercial entities in their various forms and types. An entrepreneur is skilled in the art and science of negotiation and deal-making.

Entrepreneurs thrive off those two components because being experienced in negotiating and deal-making gives you the ability you can overcome monumental hurdles that will otherwise stand in your way and stop you from reaching success. Without communication and articulation skills, you can't successfully be good at negotiating and deal-making. The great thing about today's world is that if you lack specific skills or capabilities, you can always learn them through books, courses, and the Internet. Take note, throughout this book, if you find that you lack in specific areas, the best thing to do is make haste to improve yourself.

Another thing about entrepreneurs is that we are always working on improving ourselves at all costs. Self-improvement is a part of an entrepreneur's lifestyle. We are still figuring out ways to increase our knowledge and capabilities in areas that will improve our success and enhance our businesses.

An entrepreneur's main prerogative is to know who you are. I'll touch on this concept more in the spirituality of commerce degree; however, this is a critical element of being an entrepreneur or anything you want to be in general. You must know yourself and know who you are first. Who you are is not based on your name, your societal identity, or even what you do to make a living. Knowing who you are, is about knowing yourself spiritually and mentally. You must know your strengths and weaknesses, and how you process information. You must get to know yourself as you would anyone else. Once you learn about this element of yourself and nature, being anything, including but not limited to being an entrepreneur, will become natural and comfortable. The mentality of an entrepreneur is one of strength and determination.

Money and business success are no laughing matter, especially when so many people in today's world are stuck in the muck and mire of poverty. You must have a sharp mind and be determined to secure yourself and your family in times of economic difficulty and even during economic prosperity. The grind never stops for an entrepreneur.

An entrepreneur is always looking for new ways (discovered and undiscovered) to come up; to gain more ground and traction in the business arena. An entrepreneur knows that there is no promise of tomorrow and the business market is always volatile, whether Wall Street says so or not. Therefore, an entrepreneur doesn't waste time on trivial matters. We keep what is important at the forefront of our minds so that we will always be in tune with the rapid changes ever flowing in this world. An entrepreneur is astute in creating value for others and themselves. People see entrepreneurs as someone who can add value to their lives. Learning how to create value is a paramount skill for an entrepreneur;

without it, all our efforts would be in vain. Creating value allows us to generate and attract the money that we seek to fundamentally obtain.

Creating value is essentially akin to creating great ideas, concepts, and business models. In general, creating value will be the heart and soul of your operations as an entrepreneur. Having this ability will give you a necessary edge in the business world because there are so many people in the business world who will try to use others and steal ideas and concepts for their gain. These kinds of people are parasites, and they feed off others. As an entrepreneur, you will resent parasites, and rightfully so because you will be the one creating the value; in yourself and in what you create. I will delve deeper into creating value in later degrees, but this aspect will prove to be a significant building block to your success.

Knowing how to create value gives you the power of independence so that you will not need others to create value for you. Essentially being an entrepreneur is all about being able to achieve your commercial and financial goals no matter how difficult it is. To better understand what an entrepreneur is, we must break down and examine the words, definitions, and etymology. The term hustle originally meant to move forcibly or energetically, which is not necessarily negative. An entrepreneur's primary function for themselves and others is to find ways to obtain success and make more money. It's a simple yet sophisticated activity when put into application. While others complain about finding a job, entrepreneurs just create them. An entrepreneur never complains about the economy or job scarcity.

Entrepreneurs do their best with the resources available to them at a given time. Being an entrepreneur is all about your mindset, attitude, and ability to get things done. You must have an active mentality to be an entrepreneur; without it, you will quickly give in and quit once things get a little tricky. You must maintain a positive attitude so that you are not easily discouraged when you encounter obstacles. You must also keep a balance between optimism and pessimism and be a considerable opportunist. These aspects are going to define the future of entrepreneurship. We are in an awkward place economically as Americans, and it is the entrepreneur's mission and job to see them through this period of awkwardness. Entrepreneurs are not going to sit and wait around for the economy to make a comeback. If the economy comes back, it will be because entrepreneurs created the environment for it to do so. Entrepreneurs are not waiting for politicians to pass new legislation encouraging job growth and investing in new businesses. If a new bill passes, it will be because politicians will have to keep up with the opportunities that entrepreneurs create.

An entrepreneur must be able to create meaningful and mutually beneficial business propositions for others during casual conversations. There are always opportunities to make money and that statement should be a mantra for entrepreneurs. Entrepreneurs must be ready for every opportunity to create a new deal or at least begin negotiations on making one. Negotiating is a significant skill that all entrepreneurs need to acquire. If you have this ability already, you should work on polishing it. Negotiating is significant to an entrepreneur because it allows you to create the situation and circumstance in which you can generate more streams and avenues for money to flow into your life.

In many ways, being an entrepreneur has a lot to do with being a negotiator, and being a negotiator means you must be a people person or a great communicator. You don't necessarily have to like people and be super friendly. However, you must possess the ability to relate to people on a fundamental level so that you can appeal to their vanity and sensibilities when preparing to make deals.

2nd LESSON: BECOMING AN ENTREPRENEUR

Becoming an entrepreneur is one of the most liberating things any person can do in the current financial climate. Becoming an entrepreneur will give you power and control over your commercial and business success. It allows you to create solutions to your problems. Being an entrepreneur means that you can defy the norms of the everyday working poor Americans, who think you must work hard for another person and their company; instead of rewarding yourself with your labor to start, grow and expand your own business. It is this mentality that will ensure victory in your life. King Solomon once said, "All is vanity, except that a Man works and enjoys the fruits of his labor."

If you are to work hard, it is to be for your benefit so that you can enjoy what your hard work produced. You are not to work and allow someone else to enjoy the produce of your labor. So many Americans, old and young, are nothing but mere wage slaves or just put slaves to their wages. Being an entrepreneur ensures that you will beat the rat race, and if you ever find yourself back in the rat race, you'd be able to overcome it once again.

Being an entrepreneur prepares you for adversity and difficulty in your financial life; it teaches you how to weather the storms of life. Being an entrepreneur is a skill that can easily be acquired if you set your mind to the task and focus on the essential things necessary to help you transform. This chapter will outline two crucial things about being an entrepreneur.

This degree will explain the answers to the questions of what an entrepreneur is and how to become one. After reading this degree, you will know, with certainty, whether you can become an entrepreneur and whether you have the focus and drive to train yourself to become one. It is crucial for you to take your financial life into the control of your own hands and stand firm in the reality that you will live and die by the choices you make. You must be adamant about this new fact because, throughout your entire life, you have always been the one who possessed control over your own life and the decisions you've made.

3rd LESSON:

BEING AN ACTIVE ENTREPRENEUR?

You can become an entrepreneur by merely being dedicated to entrepreneurship and financially making your way in the world. You must commit yourself to this undertaking and be determined to live the entrepreneur's lifestyle. You must first let the ideals of entrepreneurship take root in your mind and begin to feed yourself information that improves your knowledge base about entrepreneurship. Then you must take on an entrepreneur's mentality and arm yourself with knowledge about the World. The choice of becoming an entrepreneur is a life path.

It's a lifestyle; one predicated upon creating multiple streams of income for yourself. Becoming an entrepreneur takes extreme mental focus and concentration. The level of dedication you have must be second to none because it is the mental focus that will ensure your chances of success to actualize in your life. Without focus, you will achieve nothing. You cannot allow minor things to sidetrack you or distract you from your intended goals. Your level of commitment must be second to none. You must be hungry for success, so much so that you can taste it. If you are not hungry for success, then you will have nothing to draw upon internally to drive and push you when you become discouraged and feel like giving up. You must monitor your hunger for success, so your appetite doesn't become pure greed. Quite a few people think greed is okay in business, but greed can and will typically be the cause of your downfall. Greed blinds you and fogs your vision and mental focus, and you'll end up doing things that seem like the right thing to do in the short term but will destroy you in the long run. Do not be a victim of your greed; use your hunger to propel you into endeavors for tenacity and strength. An essential aspect of being an entrepreneur is intelligent and well-informed.

If you are not well informed, then the decisions you make will almost always fail. Being informed gives you the ability to make reasonable choices and gives your insight into the task at hand. Without being told, there is no chance you will have of reaching success. An entrepreneur keeps his or her ear to the streets and has their finger on the pulse when it comes to information, trends, and things in general that will help you stay on top of your game to make the best decisions possible. The main ingredient to being informed is information. We live in the information age, and in this age, information is king. Knowledge is the deciding factor regarding the success of your business endeavors. Although it is illegal, insider trading exists because traders need the latest and the most up-to-date inside scoop on what is going on with publicly traded companies, whether it may be a personal matter concerning a CEO or a massive company decision regarding profits or employees. While I do not advocate insider trading, it is important to note that an entrepreneur must treat information that can be confirmed to be correct (knowledge) as a top priority. Entrepreneurship is a challenging feat. You must be ready to stop procrastinating and allowing distractions to enter your life and take you off course. If you are a procrastinator or easily succumb to distractions, then you will never make it as a successful entrepreneur until you overcome those character flaws. Everyone has character flaws, but you must not allow your character flaws to get in the way of you and your goals; these truths are essential to becoming an entrepreneur.

Many people fail in starting a business or running businesses, and many people will continue to fail, but as the adage goes; "the race is not given to the swift nor the strong but he who endures until the end." To be a successful entrepreneur takes a tremendous amount of work ethic and character development. You can read as many self-help and motivation books and programs as you can find, but you will never achieve anything until you apply it and put it to use.

Without application, nothing you desire or want can come into existence. It takes the form of knowledge and utilization of resources to manifest that which you want to experience in your reality. Many sit back, wishing, fantasizing, and hoping their dreams come true, instead of making them come true through hard work and dedication.

I will touch on character development in later degrees of this book, but it is essential for you to know that character development is vital to becoming an entrepreneur. Another critical feature of becoming an entrepreneur is finding what you love the most and working that angle in as many possible ways. When you love doing something, it makes your experience more enjoyable. Suddenly, it doesn't feel like tedious business work or a job but more like a hobby. Don't get me wrong; you don't want to treat your business as a hobby. Taking that approach only ensures your failure, and there will always be some tedious work involved, no matter how enjoyable your endeavor is. You want to make sure you are having a good time as much as possible because maintaining that feeling will sustain your energy levels through the difficult times you will encounter. Loving what you do also increases the likelihood that you will stay dedicated to whatever you choose.

Some people can do anything and be good at it, and they will continue to pursue it because they are good. However, many people who have this capability become bored very quickly because the given tasks aren't a challenge to them. If you are one of these people, it is essential for you to find something you love or enjoy doing. On the contrary, many people are not good at most things they attempt to do. For this purpose, it is essential for you, if you fit this character type, that you find what it is you love or enjoy doing; so that you entrench yourself in that venture.

A significant part of being an entrepreneur can make self-assessments. You must be able to weigh your strengths and weaknesses and be realistic about your actual capabilities. Remember, time is money, and if you spend all your time discovering the truth about what you can and can't do, you will never have the time to execute your plans successfully and adequately make money.

4th LESSON: THE ENTREPRENEURS' PHILOSOPHY

Often, people never take the time out in their lives to reflect on the nature of the universe and how it operates. There is always more to things than what the eyes can see. There is a common thread of consciousness that connects us all to everyone, everywhere, and everything. Without understanding it in its proper context and misjudging your business endeavors, we will fail in gaining the kind of control over our lives that we are intended to have. The topic of universal consciousness is undoubtedly a subject and requires further reading and research for complete understanding, which includes the signature of quantum physics. The Spirituality of Commerce is an essential factor in being an entrepreneur. You must have an edge in your life that gives you a deeper insight into the flow of money and business. Understanding the Spirituality of Commerce gives you that idea.

Having the edge gives you the ability to make better decisions and more significant profits. Once you know how commerce operates and how spirituality coincides with it, you will be able to overcome enormous obstacles and accomplish substantial goals. A level of spirituality must be developed to be successfully satisfied on a personal level with your business endeavors. Faith and belief can be significant motivating factors in advancing your agenda and granting you a higher purpose in life, but this alone is not enough. The nature of your perception and perspective based on the spirituality of commerce and how it operates gives you a unique capability to accomplish that higher purpose in your life. Without clarity of perspective and perception, you run the risk of misjudging your business endeavors, which will undoubtedly delay you in your travels on the road to riches.

Studying spirituality will significantly increase the stability and focus of your mentality, which primarily helps you develop better plans of attack regarding your business ventures. The following degrees will outline the basics of the spirituality of commerce. It will detail what spirituality is, what commerce is, how they correlate with each other in the realm of business and how you can utilize the knowledge of its workings to your advantage in each of your business endeavors. The following degrees will show you how to apply spiritual principles in commerce and get results in a manner uncommon to most entrepreneurs.

5th LESSON: WHAT IS SPIRITUALITY?

Spirituality is the systemic ebb and flows function of energy correlating with consciousness. Spirituality is the dynamic basis for human interaction; the word spirit comes from the Greek word pneuma, which means breath. It is the energy of the breath of which we call life. Eastern Asians call this life force Chi. It is prudent for entrepreneurs to have a spiritual system to adhere to. Religious beliefs and Spiritual systems are not the same. Religion is a set of beliefs based on a specific set of dogmatic principles, whereas Spiritual policies are a set of established universal principles. Spiritual orders exist throughout religious beliefs but not vice versa.

Spiritual systems make it possible for you to focus and control your emotions, overall energy, and mentality. Spirituality provides a basis for entrepreneurs to discern their energy output as positive or negative. It allows entrepreneurs to gauge their intent behind decision-making and establishes a scale so that entrepreneurs can keep balance in their lives. Spirituality is the force that drives the physical world. It manifests itself throughout all of existence, including human activity.

Spirituality allows us to tap into our divine consciousness and pull ideas from the universal mental reservoir. This reservoir is where all thoughts and opinions come from; they come from the unlimited source of all things. From this pool, we can create what we desire. If one has a problem that needs a solution, the universal reservoir of all thoughts has the answer waiting. Spirituality gives us access to the divinity within ourselves. It provides us with the capability to reach and achieve greatness.

You will use divine consciousness if you are serious about achieving your goals. Without divine awareness, you will not know in which direction you are sailing in life. It gives you insight into the things you need to see and understand about yourself so that you may achieve your goals. Divine consciousness also allows you to reach your goals with a clear conscious because you will operate off higher principles than your average entrepreneur or person who is merely seeking to make money. Spirituality gives you the anchor you need in your life to weather the storm of obstacles you will face in life.

6th LESSON: WHAT IS COMMERCE?

The term commerce is interesting because it encompasses much of human thought and activity. More specifically, it is the exchange of energetic human potential. Many people think money itself entails the entire dynamics of commerce. However, it is only a portion of it. Money is the medium for exchanging, while trade is the activity surrounding within and without the action of exchange. Overall social relations, views, attitudes, and intellectual or spiritual are all considered commerce because it's all relative to exchanging and interchanging, which is the basis of economics. If there isn't any exchange, there isn't any commerce. An entrepreneur must have something to exchange for value or perceived value; without it, you are not able to engage in business at a beneficial level. The nature of commerce is for energy to interact and accumulate. The accumulation is relative to storing energy. The storage of this energy is called a surplus or profit. Take note that it is money that is considered currency.

In the same sense as an electrical current, currency is the basis and medium for the interchange of energy. For instance, when you think of the relation between river banks and banks and how the high seas are considered the waters of commerce. The birth of a ship, the canal, and the loading docks is all about mercantile shipping. These concepts are all grafted from the basis of commerce. These ideas are ancient and tied explicitly to all human activity, natural phenomena, and occurrences. Commerce is indeed the basis for all existence, including the action taking place in the cosmos.

7th LESSON:

HOW DOES SPIRITUALITY CORRELATE WITH COMMERCE?

The correlation between spirituality and commerce is quite profound. A more in-depth look at what spirit and spirituality are, as well as commerce, should be thoroughly and independently studied by entrepreneurs for a thorough understanding and complete comprehension of the correlation between the two. The essential relationship between spirituality and commerce is rooted in the fact that spirituality deals with the overall behavior of cosmic and terrestrial energy, while commerce deals with the behavioral nature of how this cosmic and earthly power interacts and interchange for creation and production purposes. Developing spirituality enhances your commercial experience, and commerce improves the quality and health of your spirituality. The two works in tandem with each other in a reciprocal capacity.

The spiritual aspect compliments the physical commerce that takes place. For example, the concept of giving and receiving is a universal axiom and universally applicable. This idea is essential in commerce because for one to gain something, one must give something. This constant ebb and flow relationship allows for energy to continue moving to and from when relative to transactions. The present and receive concept is primarily a spiritual concept passed down through the ages by mystics and sages of all cultures. This axiom is ingratiated into the very fabric of commerce, making it inseparable from its spiritual and commercial applications.

Many billionaires and millionaires know and understand the secret or unknown relationship between commerce and spirituality and its roots in giving and receiving. No matter what anyone says the most prominent givers or philanthropist has been and are currently the wealthiest people. The correlations between commerce and spirituality are intertwined; the definition provided in previous pages substantiates this assertion. The fourth description of commerce states that intellectual and spiritual interchange is a form of commerce. The previous description blatantly and directly specifies that spirituality and communion with the divine are indeed commerce.

When you completely understand this reality, you will never be broken again because you will realize that higher universal principles are at work when it comes to doing business in general. The very act of engaging in commerce itself is a spiritual activity. The very act of buying and selling at its root is about interchanging and exchanging, which is a spiritual activity because it is the underlying application of giving and receiving.

8th LESSON: YOUR STATE OF MIND

The most critical part of becoming an entrepreneur is the condition of your mind. Your state of mind is essential to the process of conducting business and administrating your financial affairs. It doesn't matter what we wish for, hope for, desire, need, or want; success will undoubtedly evade you if you do not have the proper state of mind. Often, we as humans emphasize our emotions, and by doing so, we overlook the importance of our mental state as the sole controller of the decisions we make. If your mind is bogged down with worries and concerns that are trivial or unfulfilling, then you will not be able to focus on the matters that need your attention. The focus is the key ingredient when determining the overall health of your state of mind. If you cannot focus and concentrate on the necessary things, then you will not be successful in your endeavors. The focus is what makes the difference between success and failure.

It is paramount that you stay away from trivial matters or thoughts that cannot benefit you in any way. The act of thinking or reasoning itself is a commercial activity consisting of buying and selling. When something presents itself to you as something you should give attention to, it is merely trying to sell you on the importance of acknowledging it. Paying attention is very relevant because we see within common language that there is a commercial value to thoughts and ideas hence intellectual property. As stated in previous degrees, energy and its dispensing and maintenance is considered commerce, but without the focus and power concentration of your mind, you will not be able to appropriately direct this energy into the appropriate things necessary to ensure your success. Paying attention to trivial matters or buying lowly valued thoughts can severely retard your ability to meet your goals and objectives because of your valuable mind power and energy on petty issues. Keeping focus is the central, most crucial aspect of achieving an efficient state of mind, capable of leading oneself to success.

Focus enables you to concentrate, and the mind is at its most potent state while concentrating on a matter, thing, or issue. To focus is to channel energy into a single thought or act. Focus enables you to zero in on whatever it is you are trying to achieve. The energy you draw on converts into motivation. Motivation empowers a person to enable oneself to do an act or thought. Motivation channels into your Focus point. Applying these actions is how you activate the very powers of self-motivation within yourself, which gives you the willpower to accomplish your goals.

This process allows you to come into control of yourself. This activity determines the overall strength of your State of Mind. The ability to focus is vital because you will always need to keep yourself motivated throughout your travels on the road to success. Without robust willpower, your actual ability, and chances to achieve your goals hinders. The state of your mind will determine the outcomes of your endeavors. Your state of mind comprises the totality of your motivation, willpower, your intent, and perspectives of optimism, pessimism, realism, and or opportunism. The key is to not hold any specific perspective dear to you, for you will find it most beneficial to know when and where to be an optimist, pessimist, realist, and or opportunist. There are a time and place for everything; therefore, be aware of your circumstances and situations because you will find it useful to know which perspective to see your event and condition through.

The best tool in your arsenal is your mind; therefore, you must use your Brain muscle to strengthen your mind. If you keep your mind sharp and enhanced; then, there will be very few situations and circumstances wherein you will not be able to solve or bring closure. Your state of mind will also determine the overall happiness of your life. Your business life will run concurrently with your personal and or love life. The more time you spend on either of them, the more likely you will likely be unsuccessful in the others. You must seek balance within your mind of the things that are most important to you. You must prioritize what will get the most of your attention and what will get the least. In the occurrence of prioritizing your care, you must also integrate all the activities of your life.

As an entrepreneur, it is imperative that you find balance in all areas of operations regarding your experience. It must be noted that balance in your life doesn't mean giving everything in your life the equal or same amount of time, energy, and attention, but rather giving those things the proper time, energy, and focus according to what it requires. These mental activities create harmony in your mind, which is very important because it gives you clarity when observing something relative to your goals and intentions. Transparency allows you to mentally see things clearly without mist or fog surrounding your thoughts. Thinking clear is paramount to having a healthy state of mind. Your state of mind is the home from where you pilot and navigate through life; you can consider it your cockpit.

9th LESSON: MEDITATION?

When dealing with matters of your state of mind, one must become aware of the variables within a situation or subject that can potentially determine the possibilities of outcomes. If you cannot harness the power of your brains and minds, then you will never be able to access the abilities of your brain and mind. Meditation helps you to acquire mastery of yourself and your mind. There are different forms of meditation, and different people use meditation for various reasons and purposes. Whether lying down, sitting, walking, running, exercising, etc., Meditation can take place. It is all about what state the mind is in, whether focused or unfocused. At certain times you may want to clear your mind of any thoughts so that answers and ideas come to you on their own, or you may want to focus and channel by concentrating on a person, place, or thing for some resolution. The activity of meditation is the same, while the goal may be different.

In the case of the latter, let's say, for example, that you have a business problem that needs a solution. Meditating by focusing and concentrating may garner a chance to see the nature of the technicalities involved in your question. Mediation gives you a new way of looking at it so that you may solve the business problem you incurred. In the same instance, if you employed the use of clearing your mind of thoughts, then you may be presented with tremendous insight that enables you to solve the business problem you had. Meditation brings you closer to your pure thoughts, untouched by outside influences.

This harmonization with yourself allows you to know yourself better and know that all solutions are within you. You just must reach for them and mine for them. Meditation enables you to do this while centering your focus and strengthening your concentration. According to Quantum Physics, meditation tunes your mind into frequencies that allow you to receive universal information within your DNA cell structure and externally from the environment around you.

Understanding the natural relationship of the world around you from a physics and quantum physics level will ultimately enable you to perceive better ways of bettering your life and your business when put into the focus of productivity. Using meditation to enhance your state of mind improves your overall experience and business endeavors. This improvement is the very process and activity of meditation itself. Relaxing and calming the mind is paramount to any mental process or action when using the deeper levels of your mind. You can access higher levels of consciousness naturally through meditation. Meditation is purely a mental exercise that activates the deeper levels of your mind and consciousness. This activity will prove to be most useful and beneficial throughout your travels on the road to success.

10th LESSON: LOVE WHAT YOU DO

Loving what you do is essential to creating a healthy state of mind and overall prosperous outcomes for your life and business endeavors. We've already seen throughout the millenniums and centuries that money does not bring happiness or security. When you love what you do, you will have no problem doing whatever it takes for you to accomplish your goals. When you love what you do, you will stay up all hours of the night and day, laboring on what you love to do. Loving what you do turns into a burning desire that is sometimes unexplainable. However, when needed, it kicks in to provide you with extra motivation to fuel your way to your goals. Loving what you do creates stability in your mind and life.

It sustains your motivation levels throughout your travels with your ventures. Loving what you do enables you to stay the course and not give up even when it seems that things may be at their worse. When you are doing what you love to do, the activity itself doesn't feel like work or difficult or unwanted labor. It feels more satisfying than anything else. It should be noted that not everyone can and will start out doing what they love to do. Some people must work on creating ventures and commercial endeavors that will increase their financial stability, which may exclude things that they love to do. Those who are not currently doing what they love to do should complete whatever it is that is keeping them from doing what they love to do and get to it as soon as possible. The sooner, the better because doing what you love to do creates more sustainable success and prosperity in your life and businesses.

The creativity that abounds when a person is doing what that person loves to do is endless and creates an environment that becomes a breeding ground for solutions, new applications, and ways of solving business problems.

When you love something, you think about it often and think of ways to express your love for it. You must apply this same mentality and emotion to what you are doing. You must immerse yourself in what you are doing if you are truly serious and focused on being successful. Without this emersion and involvement, you will never fully understand the full 720 degrees of problems and solutions with their variables and nuances, which exists within the sphere of your life and businesses. Many millionaires and billionaires have said it is the fact that they love what they do that makes them so successful in life.

Having a love for what you do is a maxim in the laws of entrepreneurship to remember throughout your travels because it is essential to the capabilities you possess to create your reality and success. There may be a time when loving what you do doesn't bring you the success you intended, in which case you must find a way to make what you love to do, provide for you financially. The message is simple: see what you love to do and find a way to turn that into a business.

11th LESSON: HOW TO RECOGNIZE AND CREATE VALUE

Recognizing and creating value is an essential usage of your mind and the strength of its state. First, you must know how to identify value, as well as how to, when, where, and why to create value. You must be aware of what value itself is and means. Value means the regard that something is held to deserve; the importance, worth, or usefulness of something and a person's principles or standards of behavior; one's judgment of what is essential in life. This definition allows you to see that the word value itself is not tangible but tangibility within the value of persons, places, or things. The science of recognizing value is the simple process of analyzing and examining the usefulness or importance of a person, place, or thing. Once you've identified this, your only task becomes to find the market and venue where it will be most valued. The more you know, the more you can do; if you have a significant or sizable amount of information to pull from your knowledge base, then you will be more familiar with the world and environment around it.

Look around you right now as you read this. Ask yourself, is there anything in your immediate or approximate space around you where someone isn't getting paid for a provided service or product through some form of legal entity? Being aware of the world and environment around you in a general sense will naturally increase your ability to recognize the value. Being able to see this allows you to see a great abundance of opportunities around you.

Witnessing this wealth enables you to access resources that others cannot because they fail to recognize value due to their limited or lack of knowledge about the world and environment around them. To enhance your perspective on being able to see abundance, you must problem-solve. Seeking solutions to problems in everyday life is always the best basis for any business model. When it comes to creating value, things are a tad bit different. Creating value where none exists can consist of two things. Number one, creating a problem and the solution would be widely known as unethical, greedy, and irresponsible. And number two, creating a solution to a problem and/or creating new perspectives of which a given person, place, or thing conducts its overall activities, from the smallest to the most extensive details. The variables involved with creating value start to minimize the more you apply technical and critical thinking to the possible outcomes of the value you are creating. When you are not only able to recognize but create value, you will never find yourself in a situation where you will not know what to do with your business. Creating value gives you the luxury of being able to develop untapped markets which didn't exist until you created them. Creativity has a significant place in business; it determines the sustainability and viability of a business endeavor.

12th LESSON: DEDICATION, DISCIPLINE & DETERMINATION

There are three attributes that every entrepreneur must assimilate into their character. These three qualities are undoubtedly dedication, discipline, and determination. These characteristics improve the constitution of your nature and the overall state of mind by imbuing strength and endurance into it. At times dedication, discipline, and determination are all you need to be able to succeed. There are many success stories where the people who have reached their goals solely by being dedicated, disciplined and determined. Adding these attributes to yourself will increase the overall quality of your character. Dedication is a feeling of firm support for or loyalty to someone or something: the quality or state of being dedicated to a person, group, cause, etc.

You must be committed to your goals and success. You must always be loyal to yourself, your ventures, and all costs within reason. Dedication gives you a sense of loyalty to your goals as missions in life. Dedication secures the importance of your goals within yourself so that you can keep a high level of commitment to what it is you are trying to accomplish. Overall, dedication makes your business endeavors highly attainable. Discipline is the second attribute that is essential in the processes of your mind. Discipline gives you the structure for which you will accomplish the goals you set. Discipline is a field of study, training that corrects, molds, or perfects the mental faculties or moral character, control gained by enforcing obedience or order, orderly or prescribed conduct or pattern of behavior, self-control, and a rule or system of rules governing conduct or activity.

Essentially discipline gives you a strict format for carrying out duties and obligations about your goals and missions. Without discipline, you will make mistakes that will bring punishment to yourself based on the activity of making bad or incorrect decisions. In many ways, you punish yourself by making mistakes and making the wrong moves.

Discipline efficiently mitigates the possible mistakes that you can make. To determine something is to cause (something) to occur in a way; be the decisive factor in and to ascertain or establish exactly, typically because of research or calculation. You must be determined to reach your goals, which gives your state of mind the ability to always create solutions for whatever problems you may face in your business. Being highly calculated in your thought processes will prove very useful precisely because it increases your level of determination through reasoning skills.

Determination provides you with a mental skill set that increases the likelihood of reaching your goals and accomplishing your missions. Determination is directly connected to motivation and self-motivation. The more motivated you are, the more determined you will be. Understanding this essential fact is crucial to creating an overall healthy and robust state of mind that is ready to apply these mental tools to become successful in his or her business endeavors.

13th LESSON: KNOW THYSELF

Knowing who you are is essential to the infrastructure of your state of mind. It gives you clarity on your perspectives and a firm foundation to build your perceptions. Without knowing who you are is a lifetime of failure and defeat. You are obliged to determine the basis of your existence in this world. Knowledge of self is paramount to self-mastery.

For it is when you completely understand and get to know yourself that you can genuinely master yourself. Once you know yourself, they say you have mastered it all. The self-mastery that accompanies your knowledge of self allows you to achieve your goals more efficiently. To honestly know yourself, you must spend time observing yourself. You must be mindful of how you respond and react to things, what you think about as well as how you feel about things, and why you choose to do the things that you decide to do. Once you have observed yourself, you will learn things about yourself that you never knew existed. Knowing yourself affords you the luxury of being able to make decisions with the utmost clarity.

Knowing who you are inside and out creates a sense of confidence that enables you to achieve your goals much more efficiently. Being an entrepreneur means you must have the full 360° knowledge of understanding your negative and positive attributes. Positive and negative are worlds unto themselves. However, they do interact with each other to create an actual plane of existence for cause and effect to manifest. Your positive or negative mindset is the same as the "atom," with its protons, electrons, and neutrons.

This trinity of sorts is no more different than that of a scale or system of balance. Therefore, you must balance the positive and negative within yourself to gain complete knowledge and understanding of yourself so that you can ultimately master and control yourself. Knowing yourself doesn't end there, though. You should know your past, present, and future. You must act to chart out and map your existence from ancestry to plans. Wanting to make money is not the only objective of an entrepreneur. An entrepreneur is interested in gaining insight into the problem, creating and applying a solution to the problem plaguing them. The most significant advantage is knowing who you are because it is only then you will recognize the real power you hold within.

14th LESSON: HOW TO STAY MOTIVATED?

Possessing the ability to motivate yourself is vital to overcoming failures and defeating the feeling of discouragement. Being self-motivated can take you places in life that you wouldn't have been able to get to without it. It is self-motivation that enables you to be dedicated, determined, and disciplined. You must be able to make yourself do things you do not necessarily want to do but perhaps must do. Motivation means movement or to move. So self-motivation intrinsically means for one to push themselves. Being able to push yourself is essential to accomplishing your goals. You are the frontline of your army and the last line of defense. Therefore, it is highly critical that you can compel yourself to apply and set yourself to tasks that further the movement towards your goals. One can never achieve their goals and accomplish their mission if they are not able to push themselves to do the things necessary to achieve those goals. As stated in previous chapters, focus is the primary element that enables you to cultivate stronger concentration, which gives you the ability to put direct energy into a specific action or activity.

Being focused is the prime mover, and all the fitness you can consider it the same as when someone turns on a car. Someone must activate the system of operation for it to begin to work. You must get to know yourself and understand what makes you work and think; what makes you do the things you do? Why do you choose the things you do? And why do you think and feel the way you do? All of this is essential because, without this collective knowledge and a basic understanding of yourself, it will be virtually impossible to motivate yourself or to be a self-motivated person. You must have your operating system per se, a system you have created for your life to function the best you see fit. Being self-motivated allows you to accomplish this because you must take direct action to bring immediate results in your life.

You will no longer daydream and wish upon a star. You must apply the tools that exist inherently within your human character and well within your range of capability to attain. There is a sense of empowerment that you feel when you can motivate, rely and depend on yourself. You must be very independent as an entrepreneur and capable of working well with others to achieve your goals.

15th LESSON: BE TOUGH ON YOURSELF

People say, "don't be so tough on yourself," the truth of the matter is that no one should be tougher on you than yourself. You should be your own worst critic. That puts your mind in a state where you can take criticism because usually, when criticism comes your way, it will only be a confirmation of that which you already know about yourself. Criticism will enable you to discern the difference between someone who is simply "hating" on you, from someone who is genuinely trying to help you. Even if someone has malicious intent with their criticism of what you are doing, you will still be able to refrain from taking it personally.

The business world can be a very unforgiving place, and you must be able to be extremely tough if you plan on lasting long and not only surviving but thriving. The world of business makes no apology for what it can do to you if you allow it. You must be able to maneuver through the business world as a ghost in a machine. You must learn to extract that which you want and need of your own will. Now, this does not condone or endorse anyone using unethical means of obtaining and extracting what they want or need.

An entrepreneur is ethical in all their pursuits. Maintaining a high standard of ethics within your entrepreneurial pursuits enables you to keep karma and dharma in your life. The strength you will develop from being tough on yourself is incomparable and second to none. Discipline, dedication, and determination are all factors that play a part in being tough on yourself. In fact, being tough on yourself will ensure that you will become a more disciplined, dedicated, and determined person. When being tough on yourself, remember not to beat yourself up over mistakes you have made in the past.

Beating yourself up is dysfunctional, and you cannot allow yourself to become a dysfunctional person. All your success rides on how well you function in the world. Being tough on yourself will help you to develop a strong character and principles. Therefore, you should make sure that you are fashioning yourself in a way that allows prosperity to flow into your life.

16th LESSON: WHAT TO DO WHEN YOU ARE DISCOURAGED?

When attempting to overcome failures, you will find yourself quickly discouraged. Being discouraged is a natural response to temporarily failing to meet an agenda or objective. It is easy to fall into despair and a myriad of other self-defeating mentalities when attempting to overcome failures. The key is knowing what to do when you're discouraged and how to handle it. When you are discouraged or feeling discouraged, you must fight through it. Do not delude yourself into believing that everything will be okay.

You must act and ensure that everything will be okay. A key component to correctly handle the feeling of discouragement is to seek out and secure friends, business associates, colleagues, and family that will encourage you when you are feeling discouraged. It is essential that you build a team of people around you that will serve as a support base for your business endeavors. I will detail and outline the necessity of building a team in later degrees. However, at this very moment, you must know what you can do yourself to defeat the feeling of discouragement.

Feeling discouraged can send you into depression, and once you're depressed, it is challenging to overcome. It is essential that you do not allow despair to seep into your life and destroy what you are trying to build. You must stop it before it gets there, and it starts with knowing what to do when you're feeling discouraged. Sometimes life can deal you blows, but that is very much the norm when you are an entrepreneur.

Being an entrepreneur can appear to many as a daunting task. However, this is the responsibility and obligation you inherit when choosing to become an entrepreneur. Discouragement is easily defeated when you have a healthy state of mind. Conviction goes a long way, as well as passion, when defeating discouragement. Discipline, determination, and dedication will prove to be handy tools when beating the feeling of discouragement. Applying many of the tools explained in previous chapters will guarantee that you can overcome the sense of discouragement. Finally, you must be able to encourage yourself and be able to push yourself because sometimes there may be no one available who can do that for you.

17th LESSON: OVERCOMING FAILURES

Failing can be negative or positive depending on what it does to you, how you take it and what you learn from it. When something doesn't work as planned, then an entrepreneur considers it a failure. The only question that remains is how you will respond to that failure. Failing is a part of living, and if taken the correct way, it will prove the best of all teachers. Although you gain a tremendous amount from failing, you do not want to become a chronic failure. Recognizing, realizing, and accepting that you will fail from time to time, you do not wish to become used to it. Failing means you are a loser, and that is something you cannot afford to be.

The reality is that you want to overcome your failures so that you negate their adverse effects on your life.

You cannot be afraid to do things that you can and will possibly fail. In other words, fear not failure itself but rather fear any intentions to fail. Overcoming failure can be extremely difficult if you are prone to self-pity and self-loathing. At times you may need to bottom out and do a little bit of self-loathing, but eventually, sooner rather than later, you must snap out of it and continue to march forward to your goals. Your dedication, discipline, and determination kicked in. The overall strength of your state of mind is what gives you the tools and ability to overcome failure in your life and business endeavors. Failure is defeated when self-motivation unites with dedication, discipline, and determination. There is no way around employing these self-perfecting attributes if one is trying to condition themselves for success, just as athletes condition the sport they'd compete.

The difficulty of overcoming failures is rooted in the lack of trust and belief in yourself and your capabilities. You cannot expect others to believe in you if you do not believe in yourself and have faith in yourself. Considering this, ask yourself if you believe you can accomplish whatever it is you want. If you can be honest with yourself, then you are one step closer to overcoming a past failure or a future one. If you are of the belief that you cannot accomplish what you want to, then you must admit it and move forward from there.

Not believing in yourself only indicates why you must convince yourself that you must believe in yourself. A significant incentive should be that no one else can do this for you, and if you don't, then you will always be stuck where you are. If you believe in yourself, your next step is to create a foundation for confidence-building strategies that gradually solve the problems that caused you to fail in the past. By setting incremental goals that lead up to resolving the overall issue of your past failures, you are efficiently formalizing your failure into a template for all future circumstances and situations of all kinds; so that solutions can be implemented according to the need and necessity. Avoiding failure and overcoming it becomes organic and spontaneous because you've already made a template of what not to do; now; now it is time to do it. Life is extraordinarily challenging, and failure is inevitable, but to minimize the feelings of self-loathing you may be susceptible to, you must adopt the mentality of a scientist so that all your activities fall within the realm of experimentation.

Focus allows for the technicalities and details as well as the logic and reason about a given matter or circumstance. Knowing is half the battle, and the other half is applying what you know. On some level applying scientific thought systems to your business endeavors will enhance its overall viability because there will be very little involved in the business endeavors that you haven't already planned for and/or determined the possible outcome.

This application makes overcoming failures as simple as one, two, or three because it will be easy for you to identify where and what you did incorrectly. You will no longer be oblivious as to why specific failures continue to reoccur. Failure is the primary obstacle you will face throughout your business endeavors. You must learn to overcome this by practicing consistency and strength in your decision-making ability.

The inability to overcome failures will significantly destabilize the foundation you are building. You do not want failure to become a routine occurrence or something you've assimilated. Failures should always be a temporary state of being and not a permanent one. The necessity to overcome failure is of utmost importance in your quest for success. You must circumvent every obstacle in your path and turn every stumbling block into a stepping-stone. The key is taking negatives and turning them into positives.

When you can execute this strategy, then you will never see failure as a result but rather the beginning of a solution and a lesson well learned. Implementing this will guarantee that you will achieve the desired results. An entrepreneur can never fail because they have mastered overcoming failure.

18th LESSON: BE A GOOD JUDGE OF CHARACTER

It may seem as if building a team is a daunting task at times. However, you must remain diligent and persevere through the scouting of potential people who could be a part of your team. Building a team also helps you develop a support system, base, and foundation.

You must possess the ability to accurately discern the characteristics of a person you are scouting for your team. Of course, no one is perfect, however (for your inner circle and in general) you should select the people with the highest skill set, abilities, and integrity. They should also have references. Building a team is much like friendships. They both take time and effort, and like all friendships and relationships, there is longevity. Trust is the most critical piece of the stability and sustainability of any relationship. Without trust, objectives and missions cannot be reached. It is trust that binds all business transactions. You must be interdependent on your team.

Interdependence is independence and dependents operating simultaneously with each other. Interdependence cannot exist without trust. You can establish trust between people who possess a high quality of ethics and principles. Mostly you must be a good judge of character, and one day hope to become a great judge of character. This vital ability alone gives you the power to effectively and efficiently choose whom to allow in your inner circle. Your inner circle is sacred; therefore, it should only consist of people you trust. You must have a discerning eye. Being able to discern people, their actions, their abilities, how they do things, and even how they think gives you a distinct advantage when you are scouting for potential members for your team.

Also, building a team consist of socializing on a personal level; it is essential for people to know and understand that you are professional and always ready to handle business. Taking care of business and implementing solutions will make your team trust you. Make sure the team you are building understands the vision you have for your business; many business plans have been thwarted because of poor communication between the team members and the entrepreneur.

19th LESSON: BUILDING A TEAM

You've probably heard this before, "you cannot do it alone." You should not take this statement for granted. It is one of the simplest things to grasp when dealing with the realm of entrepreneurship. It is imperative and essential that you build a team that will help you reach your goals. A team will enable you to achieve things you wouldn't have accomplished without them.

I cannot stress enough how important this aspect of being an entrepreneur is. Without a team, you won't get very far in business. You may even have superior multi-tasking abilities; however, being proficient in multi-tasking isn't enough to meet all the requisites required for insured success for your business.

In general, a team can consist of a combination of employees, partners, vendors, sellers, professionals, family, friends, loved ones, etc. it's all about finding the balance between what you want and what you need. You will find yourself building multiple teams for multiple purposes. Even then, you will still need a core team, or what Napoleon Hill calls a "Mastermind Group." A mastermind group is tough to build. It may take years for you to complete the building of your mastermind group. Even then, you will have team members who resign or perhaps remove from your mastermind group. You may even add new members to your team from time to time. Building a team, i.e., a mastermind group, is always a work in progress. In my early years as an entrepreneur, I always thought I didn't need anyone to do anything for me or assist me. I thought I could do it by myself and didn't need anyone. Besides, whenever I'd try to include someone in my plans or assist me on a specific task, I always said to myself, "I could have done this myself." At times I may have been correct, but often I was wrong.

I will admit that building a team is not easy. You may have to deal with your team members' personal issues, business issues, financial issues, etc., or at the very least, whatever may be taking place in their lives, could potentially be a risk and a threat to your overall team. These are some of the things to consider when you're assessing the prospects of building a team.

20th LESSON: ORGANIZE YOUR LIFE

When organizing your life, you must take inventory of what it is you are currently doing and what you plan on doing. Organization calibrates your life in such a way that allows you to operate very efficiently when executing solutions and plans. The key is to integrate all the many facets relative to your life so that achieving synergy is complete. Achieve synergy, and systemic spontaneity will ensue. Essentially you are dynamically creating an environment around yourself, wherein you will meet potential people to add to your team randomly, regularly, and consistently. When your life is organized, all your activities coincide with socializing to some degree or another. It doesn't matter if you are purchasing something online or speaking with the cashier at your local grocery store; you are still socializing because you are interfacing with other people.

An entrepreneur and those aspiring to be one should have their lives organized around their business ideas and plans. An entrepreneur should have a banking team, investment team, financial team, legal team, spiritual team, health team, security team, and personal team. As you organize your life to achieve maximum efficiency when pursuing business endeavors, you will undoubtedly have to deal with the previously stated paradigms so that you can reach success. As an entrepreneur, you must view yourself as a monarch, a King or Queen, and everyone on your team comprises your house of nobles. In the world of business, you must be decisive; there is no time for second-guessing. So, it is imperative that you organize your life so that you can take advantage of opportunities that you will frequently come into contact with.

Once you organize your life, you will be able to see all the things you will need to succeed. You will see all the tools, people, places, and things you can utilize on your road to success. At this juncture, many people fail to do this successfully, which is to examine their motivations and intent before deciding to take specific actions. Organizing your life adds tremendous benefits to your overall life, specifically your business.

21st LESSON: THINGS YOU SHOULD KNOW

If you make the great leap into being an entrepreneur in today's geopolitical and socioeconomic construct, there are some essential things you must know. There are things taking place around the world and in the greater society that directly and indirectly affects our situations and circumstances. As an entrepreneur, you are obligated to know the specifics of the world of business, politics, and how people work. You must make moves and act based on the best information available at the time. The more you know, the more you can do. Never forget that because it is always with the knowledge that you can begin to apply it and transform it into power. You must become active and aggressive towards obtaining useful and vital information.

Your smartphone should have apps that bring help you gain knowledge; this is essential to your overall game plan. You must study and observe the world's geopolitical climate and socioeconomic constructs. Information will help you make more informed decisions about your business and personal life. You must also remember that the world has an integrated global economy. We are more interdependent and connected to one another globally than we have ever been in the past. Being connected the way we are, suggests that there is a world of opportunity. You must see the world as one big marketplace, with submarkets being represented by the various countries and governments that house them. The more you know about these markets and submarkets, the more opportunities you will have to participate in them. As an entrepreneur, it is imperative that you have knowledge of information and access to the endless markets that exist on this planet.

An entrepreneur sees his local neighborhood as equally valuable as someone else's local neighborhood living 6000 miles away. Technology has connected us in such a way that we have access to all markets internationally at the click of a button. This kind of interconnectivity that exists globally removes the ability to make excuses for not accessing and taking advantage of opportunities that exist globally.

22nd LESSON: CERTIFICATIONS VS COLLEGE DEGREES

College for many young people around the world has become unaffordable and unattainable. In first-world countries, the value of a college degree dropped dramatically and drastically. Those with college degrees are finding themselves out of work for being over-qualified, unqualified, or laid off because of company downsizing. As an entrepreneur, you must decide if college is for you or not. College degrees which can take four years or more, can significantly stifle how much you can achieve in the real world while pursuing a four-year degree and racking up expenses, student loans, and tuition fees. I'm not saying you should not pursue a college degree, but not everyone needs a college degree. A college degree is still very much relevant as it pertains to the STEM fields (which I will go into more detail about in later degrees) and professional services such as lawyers, doctors, accountants, etc. Everyone else who is not pursuing jobs and those specific fields, blue-collar vocational skills and entrepreneurship are the remaining alternatives. By the time someone graduates college, the world has usually changed drastically, and the major for which you may have a degree may be utterly useless after you graduate due to rapid industry transformation and the release of new technology. Which brings us to the question, which is better; a certification or a four-year degree?

As stated, four-year degrees previously in fields where there are still industries to support them are very vital to the primary function of society and, therefore, still very useful.

However, certifications offer an individual the option to choose what skill set they want to learn. Certification enables an individual to acquire a set of skills they can provide as services, either employed or self-employed. Certifications usually take six months to complete or at least no more than one year. Companies today are looking to minimize unnecessary employees. Why pay five people to do something you can outsource and pay a consultant or specialists to do it? Once the company outsources or pays the consultant/specialist, the employer doesn't have to pay health insurance or any other employee benefit. In corporate America, that is the general logic of why layoffs and job loss occur.

It's time for the individual, specifically those living in first-world countries, to re-examine their interests and society and how they plan to secure their financial future and current situation. Obtaining certification is much more flexible, and each one you complete will provide you with sufficient and recognized certification. The more certification you have, the more jobs and businesses will be available to you. Take, for instance, corporate event planning. You can take a course that is acknowledged and accredited to give certification in corporate event planning and have one of the highest-paid jobs and/or businesses in America. Companies are looking for more top corporate event planners, and they are looking to hire certified and corporate event planning consultants. Now there are many colleges that offer these certification courses, which makes the battle between certifications and four-year degrees real. From a personal trainer to a business coach, a myriad of free and paid certifications will advance your skill set. As an entrepreneur, you'll find it most useful to acquire as many certifications as you deem necessary, because you want to learn something new.

23rd LESSON: FUNDING YOUR VENTURES

A major obstacle that many entrepreneurs find most challenging is the ability to fund ventures. Funding your business can still be extremely challenging, but at the heart and soul of your ability to be a successful entrepreneur. If you are not able to secure the financing of your endeavors, they will never come to fruition in all reality. They will remain ideas and things that you want to do. Being able to fund your ventures takes them from the realm of thought and brings them into the realm of reality. There are many ways to finance your business, but I will just give you some basic tips.

As an entrepreneur, proper credit is vital to your success. Having credit allows you access to preliminary capital in the form of credit cards, personal loans, and a myriad of other types of financing. Even when you begin to build business credit, initially, you will have to be a personal guarantor for all credit and loan agreements for your company.

Having credit gives you the advantage of being able to experiment with your business without risking anyone else's money initially. This tactic is especially useful for those persons who lack the necessary tools and resources to secure financing. If you do not have credit, you should initially begin funding your ventures by repairing your credit and getting it into a high standing. There are numerous ways to remove negative items from your credit report. Familiarize yourself with the federal laws concerning credit.

There are two federal acts relating to consumer laws and credit. The first path to changing your life is acquiring knowledge that will enable you to overcome obstacles and achieve your goals. Having excellent credit is your first immediate access point to capital. Credit primarily is based on your word in the bond system; you are signing your good name into agreements where a merchant is providing you with debt. What you choose to do with your credit will determine how you can access capital. Most people use that credit to buy things they cannot afford, however as an entrepreneur, you will use this capital access point to secure financing for preliminary expenses of your ventures. Before going full throttle and head-first into a business venture, you will need funds to pay for some minor and significant costs. You will need to incorporate all form a business entity that will cost you money whether you have a job or not; if you have access to capital through credit, that would be a wise purchase; because you are spending your credit to create an opportunity to make more money and not just consume.

Another instance in which your credit will be advantageous is for securing personal loans, business loans, leasing equipment, renting, and even investing. In the case of financing, if you have a considerable sizable credit line, you can take a portion of that and invest in the Crypto Currency, Forex market, stock options markets, futures market, precious metals market, and real estate market. With today's technology, all of this can be controlled right from the palm of your hand.

You can become your investor and control all your investments. When you know how to make money and can manage money, which is the responsibility, obligation, and duty of all entrepreneurs. Then you'll be in the driver's seat for the duration of your ventures; you should eventually want your investments taking care of your daily living expenses. In other words, you want to develop residual income so that you can be free to pursue your entrepreneurial endeavors. Once you secure your daily living expenses, then you will not need to worry about.

being desperate to be successful in your ventures. Another excellent source of financing and funding your ventures is crowd-funding. Crowd-funding is also somewhat of a by-product of social media. Crowd-funding allows you to present your adventure or project to the public and solicit them for investment. Until recently, people could not directly invest in the crowd-funded campaign.

They could only get some memorabilia, product, or something that indirectly showed they donated to the crowd-funded campaign. It was off-limits to the general investment market, investors had to be accredited, and you would have had to pass the S.E.C. standards and regulations for going public.

The SEC and the Obama administration have signed a law granting crowd-funded campaigns to market to the public, non-accredited investors included. Congress passed the Jumpstart Our Business Startups (JOBS) Act in 2012. The JOBS Act allows any person, whether an accredited investor or not, to invest up to $25,000 in any small business. Crowd-funding allows you to link with the minds of people who see your vision and are interested in the product or service you are presenting to the public. There are many more ways to fund your ventures. However, if utilized and maximized, the ones that have been provided can take care of about half of the initial funding your ventures will cost. Many people say, "never invest your own money, always use other people's money," this can and will serve to be a useful tool; however, being self-sufficient is the entrepreneur's way of doing things.

24th LESSON: UNIFORM COMMERCIAL CODES

If you are going to maneuver through the seas of commerce, then it is essential that you understand the uniform commercial codes. The uniform commercial code is a set of international laws acted by the governments of the world, based on the law of merchants and the law of nations. The UCC governs the nature and transactions of all contracts and commerce in general. The legal scholars of the world constructed the UCC. They examined ancient and modern treaties, contracts, agreements, as well as international case law; to create the basis and foundation for the existence of the uniform commercial code.

As far as the United States is concerned, the UCC has been enacted in every state of the union's statutes. The UCC governs every agreement and/or transaction, private and/or public. Studying and applying uniform commercial codes will significantly increase your knowledge and understanding of commerce. It will enhance your negotiating skills and solidify your ability to make deals.

As an Entrepreneur, negotiating and making deals is a large part of what you do. You must have these tools in your toolbox for entrepreneurship. Uniform Commercial Code covers a wide range of subject matter relating to commerce; from the process of offers and refusal, sales, and refunds, to shipping, notes, and receipts, the Uniform Commercial Code covers it all. The laws of commerce govern everything in our society. According to the federal code of regulations, all crimes are considered commercial. Everything that transpires within society or nature consists of a transaction. The Uniform Commercial Codes are the tools we humans developed so that we may have consistent and reliable means to transact with one another.

The UCC also consists of a series of actions and counteractions that commercial users can apply to their given situation. Everything from notes, stocks, bonds, securities, and pretty much all forms of paperwork, including the nature and application of offer/acceptance and non-acceptance. There isn't any form of business that one can do wherein the UCC will not apply. Applying Uniform Commercial Codes to your state of mind an outlook on commerce can and will significantly increase your maneuverability and navigation through the seas of commerce. The Uniform Commercial Codes are rules and guides that Entrepreneurs assimilate into their arsenal of tools to be used when transacting business.

This book has outlined the first 24 Lessons of the entrepreneur's Philosophy. This book is the first of several others that are soon to follow. After reading these degrees, you should be able to begin your journey of entrepreneurial success. Be brave, be smart and build your commercial empire.